WOLF STRACHE

Forms
and Patterns
in Nature

PANTHEON BOOKS

A Division of Random House

NEW YORK

DESCRIPTIVE LIST OF PLATES BY HORST JANUS

TRANSLATION BY FELIX KAUFMANN

With the exception of the plates named below, all photographs in this volume have been taken by Dr. Wolf Strache with a Leica camera and Leica lenses. The following institutions and photographers contributed photographs for this book: Plate 2, Kosmos-Press; plate 3, Deutsches Museum, München; plate 5, Ryukichi Shibuya; plates 6, 10, 19, 30, 31, Ullstein; plate 7, Nationaal Foto Persbureau; plates 8, 9, Photogrammetric, München; plate 11, Emil Brunner; plate 12, Sabena; plate 13, Pawli; plate 14, Alfred Ehrhardt; plate 43, Shoji Ueda; plate 16, Storz; plate 23, Keystone; plates 26, 27, Prof. William Guertler; plate 33, Horst Kratz-mann; plates 34, 49, 50, Dr. Horst Janus; plates 35, 86, Anton Stankowski.

Copyright © 1973 by Random House, Inc.

Copyright © 1956 by Pantheon Books, Inc.

All rights reserved under International and Pan-American Copyright Conventions. Published in the United States by Pantheon Books, a division of Random House, Inc., New York, and simultaneously in Canada by Random House of Canada Limited, Toronto. Re-issue, book first published by Pantheon Books in 1956.

Library of Congress Cataloging in Publication Data
Strache, Wolf, 1910—
Forms and Patterns in Nature.
Reprint of the 1956 ed. published by Pantheon,
New York, with one new illus.
  1. Natural history—Pictorial works. 2. Nature photography. I. Title.
[QH46.S79 1973]   779'.3'0924   73—3468
ISBN 0—394—42541—3
ISBN 0—394—70974—8 (pbk)

Manufactured in the United States of America

Reprint Edition

Front cover photo: Aerial photo of creek system (see plate 7).

Back cover photo: Pinions of Argus pheasant (see plate 79).

Contents

Preface

As we look at the plates in this book we soon make a curious discovery: Nature uses the same ideas in her forms and patterns in quite different places. Inexhaustible though Nature is in designing shapes, she may use the same design in various aspects—on a large scale and on a small scale, in minerals and in plants, in animals and in the immense spaces of the earth and the sky. The aerial photograph of a river estuary resembles a plant with its stem, its leaves, and its flowers, and the forked lightning striking from the sky displays a similar branching pattern. The foot of the mushroom coral has the same arrangement of lamellae as the underside of a mushroom. Both butterflies and birds are adorned with gleaming peacock's eyes. The bone tissue of a sheep looks similar to the fur of the jaguar. It is one of the special pleasures of the naturalist and the photographer to discover these parallels in different realms of creation. And this book, which purposely limits itself to black-and-white reproductions, may assist in tracking down these secret designs of Nature. For who would deny that there is an astonishing formal resemblance between the skeleton of the star coral and the stars formed by hoar frost on the leaves of a stonecrop, or that the cross-section of a spine of the sea urchin seems closely akin to the world of radiolarian shapes? Naturally, the scientist must reject the idea of true kinship as an explanation of the similarity of all these phenomena.

And yet another discovery strikes the observer: human imagination, too, so it would seem, draws on the same store of patterns that Nature uses for her purposes. Gothic cathedrals were decorated with beautiful rosettes long before a human eye looked through a microscope at the artistic arrangement of rays in a diatom. And yet the stained glass looks as if it were copied from the microscopic picture. The delicate lattice work of the glass sponges resembles a miraculous lace doily. Snails and sea-shells bear ornaments of the kind we design for our china. And in many forms evolved by Nature the lines and shapes of contemporary modern art are anticipated; yet it is unlikely that Picasso studied the feeding patterns of the microlepidoptera larvae before putting an abstract composition on paper. Many designs discovered here by the camera could be taken over without change in the design of modern textiles, and those who would see and wear them would think them beautiful and appropriate. Nature provides excellent models even in the sphere of modern arts and crafts.

The pictures in this book show a tiny fragment of the world of the visible and of the seemingly invisible, brought to the eye by the camera and by the modern possibilities of photography. Part of the plates we owe to the new view of the earth seen from an airplane. The views of distant portions of the sky were obtained in the observatories of the U.S.A. with their giant telescopes. The vast majority of the exposures were made by the Leica camera and its interchangeable lenses, above all with close-up attachment and mirror reflex—an equipment that serves better than any other both to bring the macrocosm nearer to the eye and to allow the recording even of the very smallest things with high precision. Thus for all photographs taken by the editor himself, the Leica was used exclusively.

Wolf Strache

Descriptive List of Plates

SKY AND EARTH

1 STAR TRACKS

If a stationary camera is focused on the pole star at night and the shutter opened for an extended period, the individual stars are recorded as segments of a circle, owing to the rotation of the earth. In the case of our picture the exposure time was about five hours. Even the varying degrees of brightness of the different stars are demonstrated by this method.

2 SPIRAL NEBULA IN THE CONSTELLATION OF THE GREYHOUNDS OF HELVETIUS (CANES VANATICI)

Spiral nebula is a term derived from the optical impression we receive of stellar systems with spiral or elliptic structure. All of them lie far outside our own galactic system and, like the spiral nebula depicted here, can be seen only by means of telescopic mirrors or lenses. The sole exception is the nebula nearest to us, in the constellation Andromeda, which can be seen with the naked eye at a distance of about 800,000 light years.

3 GASEOUS NEBULA IN THE CONSTELLATION OF THE SWAN

Gaseous nebulae are diffuse and irregular and emit light. According to the source of this light two types are distinguished. In emission nebulae free atoms and molecules radiate light, while in reflection nebulae the light of the stars is reflected by interstellar matter. Frequently both types of light occur mixed.—Gas nebulae always belong to our own galaxy.

4 SOUTHERN PART OF THE MOON WITH CRATERS

The earth's moon still presents many problems to us. Thus even its origin is by no means clear: it may have been captured by the earth or thrown off by it. There are also different theories to account for the development of its surface. But it is established that the moon has no atmosphere, which is what makes possible its optical exploration. That is why its surface structures, the "seas," mountain ranges, craters, annular mountain groups, depressions and crevices are quite well known through observation and photography with lens and mirror telescopes.—The picture shows a section of the moon at the time of the last quarter, photographed through the world's largest mirror telescope in Mount Wilson observatory.

5   FLEECY CLOUDS

Cloud formations that look like lambs' fleeces are usually cirri; but they also occur as alto-cumulus clouds, as in the picture. As cirri they float at a height of about 20,000 feet and consist of ice particles; while the alto-cumulus fleeces are found only at about 15,000 feet and mostly consist of super-cooled water droplets.

6   FORKED LIGHTNING

Lightnings are spark discharges equalizing electric tensions. Usually this equalization takes place inside a thundercloud, much more rarely between a thundercloud and the earth. In the latter case lightning "strikes," with well-known consequences.—Tension and current of lightning discharges are always very high (about 100 million volts and 10,000 ampères). However since the time for the discharge is very short (a fraction of a millisecond), the energy turnover is comparatively low (a few hundred kilowatt hours).

7   CREEK SYSTEM

Aerial photographs also serve to point up patterns under water, such as the ramifications of a creek system. Creeks are natural channels formed by the flow of the tides in shallow portions of the sea. Even at the lowest ebb, however, they remain under water.

8   DRIFT ICE AT THE COAST OF FRANZ JOSEPH LAND

Above are clouds, below drift ice. Between sky and earth hovers a zeppelin from which this snapshot was taken during a polar flight. (Drift ice presents an insidious danger to navigation and has been responsible for many a shipwreck).

9   JUNGLE RIVER IN NEW GUINEA

This photograph was taken from an airplane flying at 15,000 feet. From this height the meanderings of a large river appear only as tiny loops. Such photographs are used for surveying inaccessible areas; the one reproduced here comprises 170 square miles. This survey method is called photogrammetry.

10   COLORADO CANYON

The imposing erosion landscape of the Grand Canyon area presents this characteristic ornamental effect to an oblique bird's-eye view. It is due mainly to the stratification which is visible throughout and to the terraces and loops formed by the Colorado River. The river itself can only be seen in one place near the center of the picture. In the course of its long history it has eaten its way into the rock for more than a mile deep in a few places.

11   SAND DUNES IN THE SAHARA DESERT

A cursory inspection of this picture would fail to provide information about its scale. For the sand gives rise to exactly the same patterns, whether it is blown about by the wind on a large scale or on a small scale. But when we look more closely, the tufts of the palms give an indication of the scale of the sand formations, and also of the catastrophic effects driftsand can have on oases in the desert.

10

12 CRACKS IN DRY MUD

When surface layers of the soil are subjected to intensive drying, cracks appear which form a network that grows increasingly denser as desiccation proceeds. In the picture it is easy to recognize the area that was occupied by the last puddle before it dried up. During the further course of drying more cracks will appear even in this area.

13 ICE FORMATION ON A RIVER

The freezing of water never proceeds simultaneously across the whole surface. In a river, ice formation begins at the banks. Floes of ice detach themselves and form large sheets in which they are joined together by thinner ice. When the thaw sets in, the melted ice on the surface forms an intricately branched system of channels.

14 RIPPLE MARKS IN SHALLOW SEA

The mud at the bottom of shallow water becomes rippled in a regular manner by the play of the surface waves. These ripple marks run at a right angle to the direction of the waves: they are flat on the side of the wind and steep on the side away from it. On land similar formations can occur in sand dunes; even petrified ripple marks have been found.

15 REFLECTION ON MOVING WATER

Every water surface is in constant motion. Even the smoothest sea is subject to small distortions because the air, too, is never at rest. These movements of the water are demonstrated most clearly when an image is reflected by it. Reflection of a light source gives rise to pictures such as this, the striation of which is reminiscent of the structure of an agate.

16 FOAM FORMATION ON WATER

The water of lakes and ponds, brooks and rivers, and especially that of the sea, is not chemically pure. Apart from various salts it contains also organic substances in solution, e.g., albumin. In a manner exactly analogous to the beating of egg-white, the beating of the waves causes this to form foam on the surface.

THE MINERALS

17 ROCK CRYSTAL

Crystals are the form in which solid matter normally occurs. The atoms and molecules in every crystal are arranged in a geometric order, the so-called crystal lattice. This finds its visible expression in the shapes of crystals all of which can be reduced to one of six systems: regular, hexagonal, quadratic, rhomboidal, monoclinic and triclinic. Rock crystal, SiO_2, belongs to the hexagonal system.

18 PYRITES CRYSTALS

These crystals are beautiful regular cubes, but the same mineral also occurs in pentagon dodecahedras. That is the name for a solid bounded by twelve pentagons. Chemically, pyrites is FeS_2. It is a widely distributed mineral. Beside pure sulfur it is the most important raw material for the manufacture of sulfuric acid. Because of its yellow metallic sheen it has often been taken for gold. Hence its popular name "fool's gold."

19 BASALT COLUMNS

Basalt is a volcanic rock consisting of plagioclast, augite and magnetite. The characteristic columns were formed during the cooling of the melted rock. They have a polygonal cross-section and stand at right angles to the plane of cooling.

20 FLUORSPAR

This belongs to the halide minerals, the name for naturally occurring salts of the metals K, Na, Ca, Mg, Cu, et al. with the halogens F, Cl, Br, I. Fluorspar has the chemical formula CaF_2 and occurs in several regular holohedral varieties (cube, octahedra) and their combinations. It can be shiny like glass, colorless, yellow-green or blue, and anything between transparent and opaque. It is a raw material for the manufacture of hydrofluoric acid which is used for etching glass.

21 POLISHED AGATE SURFACE

Agates are hydrated quartzes (SiO_2) in a non-crystalline (amorphous) state. They consist of layers of different quartzes, usually of different colors, often found filling cavities in rocks. From the outside they usually look dull and uninteresting; only by polishing them in the right plane the beauty of their structure and their colors is brought out.

22 CALCSPAR CRYSTALS

Calcspar ($CaCO_3$) occurs in many different crystal forms, all of which belong to the hexagonal system. As dense limestone, chalk, or granular marble it forms enormous sedimentary layers. Beautiful crystals, such as those depicted here, are found in many places in cavities in basic volcanic rocks. Water-clear calcspar crystals display the phenomenon of double refraction, i.e., in refracting a ray of light they separate it into two rays whose planes of vibration are at right angles to each other.

23 STALACTITES

These are found in caves where water rich in calcium bicarbonate drops down from the roof. As the water and carbon dioxide evaporate, calcium carbonate precipitates and forms slowly growing stalactites hanging down from the roof and stalagmites growing upward from the floor of the cave. Occasionally a stalagmite and a stalactite grow together to form a column.

24 VARIEGATED MARBLE

Marble in the strict sense is calcspar, chemically $CaCO_3$, granular in structure and crystallized in the hexagonal system, but only hemihedrally. The marble quarried at Carrara (Italy) is the most beautiful, because it is quite pure. Loosely speaking, other crystalline limestones are also referred to as marble, for instance the rhomboidally crystallized aragonite depicted here. The variegation is due to the presence of other chemical compounds, such as oxides of iron.

12

25 NATROLITH

This is a silicate mineral resembling the feldspars. It has a high water content and is usually found in the cavities of volcanic rocks. Natrolith belongs to the rhomboidal system; it is usually fibrous-white, occasionally also with a colored border, as in the picture.

26 POLISHED METAL SURFACE

This very highly magnified picture shows the surface of an alloy consisting of 80% lead, 15% antimony and 5% tin. That is the composition used to make type metal for printing. The softness of the lead is modified by the addition of some hardening antimony, which raises the melting point only slightly.

27 POLISHED METAL SURFACE

The metal in this picture is also an alloy, of 72% copper, 19% sulfur, and 9% lead. The high magnification reveals a coarse structure, an indication of low tensile strength.

28 MENTHOL CRYSTALS

Menthol, chemically hexahydrothymol $C_{10}H_{19}OH$, normally crystallizes in shiny colorless prisms. The form in the picture was obtained by crystallization from a few drops only, and is incomplete. Menthol has a strong peppermint odor, imparts a sensation of coolness to the skin, and allays itching. It is hardly soluble in water, but dissolves easily in alcohol, ether, and essential oils. It is best known from its use in cough pastilles.

29 CRYSTALS OF SALT OF SORREL

Salt of sorrel is an acid potassium oxalate $C_4O_8H_3K$. It is poisonous. Commercially it is available as white opaque crystals or as a finely crystalline powder. Its name is derived from the old method of preparing it by evaporating sorrel juice. Today it is manufactured synthetically for the removal of rust and inkspots and as a mordant in textile printing.

30 SAL AMMONIAC CRYSTALS

From a few drops of solution ammonium chloride, NH_4Cl, pine-needle shapes like these shown here crystallize, forming a white salt, very soluble in water, with a bitter-salty taste. Its peculiarity is that it sublimes; i.e., on heating it passes from the solid to the gaseous state without melting. Its uses are manifold, as artificial manure, for soldering, in batteries, for refrigeration and various other purposes.

31 METOL CRYSTALS

Metol is the sulfate of paramethylaminophenol $HOC_6H_4NHCH_3$. It is used as a developer for photographic films, often in combination with other substances, e.g., with hydroquinone. Crystal formations of this kind are often found in developing dishes that have not been rinsed.

32 FROST CRYSTALS ON A WINDOW

Crystallization of water vapor on glass panes can give rise to manifold shapes, according to conditions prevailing during their growth. Large "flowers" are formed if the surrounding air cools slowly, but the crystals which are formed if frost sets in suddenly are small. Humidity and purity of the air also have a great influence; in dust-free air the crystals exhibit more regular growth. They belong to the hexagonal system, like quartz.

THE PLANT WORLD

33 AUTUMN LEAVES

Every fall the ground of the forest is covered again with fallen leaves. First the leaves wilt on the tree, allowing their valuable contents to flow back into the storage organs of the tree. Then a separation layer is formed near the base of the stalk where separation occurs. A leaf scar remains behind which is closed by lignified tissue and cork. No new leaf can ever grow at that same spot.

34 SPIRAL ALGAE (SPIROGYRA)

These are green unbranched filaments. Each cell of the filament has a nucleus and one or more ribbon-shaped chloroplasts which wind spirally along the inner wall. In this way the chlorophyll is distributed over a large surface. This is of great importance for efficiency in photosynthesis. Growth of the alga takes place lengthwise, followed by transverse cell division and by further elongation.

35 MALVA FLOWER

Not only the leaves, but even the petals have a richly branching network of veins. For both are dependent on ample supplies of water and nutritive substances to all parts. Only the veins of the petals are much finer, as they do not have to contribute to structural rigidity to the same degree as those in the leaves.—The petals are modified stamina, as is clearly recognizable in many "double" flowers.

36 GRAIN OF ASH WOOD (FRAXINUS)

According to the plane of section through the wood the structural elements appear quite differently. The picture shows a longitudinal section through the axis of the trunk. The annual rings appear vertical in this way, each year being made up of a dark porous and a lighter smooth layer. The porous layer represents the growth in spring and early summer when a great volume of sap rises up in the tree through wide vessels. The darker horizontal stripes are the medullary rays through which interchange takes place between inner and outer tissues.

37 CROSS-SECTION OF YEW TRUNK (TAXUS)

This cross-section shows quite a different aspect from the longitudinal section in the last picture. Here the annual rings are darker and lighter concentric circles. It is easy to calculate from them at which age the distortion of the trunk began. The causes for the distortion are more difficult to ascertain; they are usually very complex. The medullary rays are barely visible in the cross-section. They run radially. The cracks appeared while the wood dried out.

38 LEAVES OF DATE PALM (PHOENIX)

Leaves as finely branched as these from a date palm are called pinnated, from the Latin word for feather. The plant begins by growing an undivided leaf surface which is folded like a fan. But before the leaf unfolds long strips of tissue die off along the folds, leading to the characteristically branched leaf area.

39 FRUCTIFICATION OF CLEMATIS

Clematis is a woody plant which uses the stalks of its leaves for climbing. Its white flowers are arranged in loose clusters, and every flower gives rise to a number of fruits. After maturation the seeds are scattered by a flying mechanism, which develops from the styles of the flower after fertilization. They grow into feathery haired appendages which help the seeds to be borne by the wind.

40 BEGONIA LEAVES

The Begoniaceae are distinguished by an oblique structure of the leaf which is developed quite differently on each side of the main vein. The flowers, too, are asymmetrical.—Begonia displays a peculiar kind of regeneration. If a leaf is cut off and placed on moist sand, roots develop on the stalk of the leaf. In addition the leaf itself gives rise to new plantlets, especially after the veins are severed. This method can be used for the asexual (vegetative) reproduction of Begonia plants.

41 HOAR FROST ON STONECROP (SEDUM)

While a green plant is active a continuous stream of water flows through it. The water is absorbed by the roots and most of it is given off by the microscopically small stomata of the leaves. This process is most intensive in daytime, but it does not cease even at night. If the air temperature is below freezing-point, the water vapor is condensed instantaneously and freezes to ice. If the moisture in the air freezes out on a large scale extensive hoar frost deposits are formed.

42 SURFACE OF A CACTUS (CACTACEAE)

Cactaceae are extensively adapted to a dry habitat. For this purpose the evaporating surface area is kept as small as possible. Thus leaves are missing, or rather transformed into the kind of thorns visible in the picture. This also affords good protection against feeding animals. The hairs, which are also visible, further reduce transpiration by keeping a layer of air in close contact with the plant surface. In addition the stem is covered by a thick cuticle with few stomata. Its interior is equipped for storage of water. These features serve to adapt the Cactaceae for life in deserts and on dry sandy soil. The botanists call such plants xerophytes.

43 DECAYING ARTICULATION OF A PRICKLY PEAR (OPUNTIA)

The vessels of this portion have resisted decomposition longest because their walls are lignified. Beside conduction their function is also to give rigidity to the plant. In order to supply all parts of the shoot they are joined by multiple connections. Such connections are called anastomoses.

44 BANANA LEAF (MUSA)

The rim of a banana leaf is intact by nature, as shown here. But as these leaves do not, like most other leaves, have a reinforced rim, the wind soon breaks the leaf surface along the depressions.—Botanically speaking, the banana plant is a perennial herbaceous plant. Its tree-like appearance is due to the leaf stalks which are rolled round one another to form a pseudo-trunk.

45 LEAF SKELETON OF THE BLACK POPLAR (POPULUS)

The areas of all leaves are traversed by veins, which serve to conduct fluids and to give rigidity to the leaf. The main vein runs on the left side near the top of the picture; it is continuous with the leaf stalk. Finer branch veins spread from it on both sides; these in turn have still finer branches. All have multiple connections with each other. The last and finest branches end freely. A reticulum of veins like the one depicted here is typical of dicotyledonous plants. In monocotyledonous plants the veins run parallel to each other.

46 SCALY BARK ON THE TRUNK OF A PLANE TREE (PLATANUS)

Bark is the encasing tissue of stems and roots in woody plants. Supplies of water and nutritive substances do not reach this outermost layer, so that it dies off. As the trunk grows in width the bark cracks and splits off. By that time the lower-lying tissues have developed sufficiently to become the new bark. The bark forms a protective coat round the wood. For one thing it protects against water loss and temperature fluctuations, for another the tannins contained in the bark afford protection against decay.

47 MOTTLED LEAF OF A BEGONIA

Begonias and other garden plants often display whitish-gray spots on their green leaves, such as those seen here and also on the begonia on plate 40. These spots lack the green pigment chlorophyll by means of which the plant harnesses light energy to build carbohydrates from carbon dioxide and water. Such hereditary depigmentation is called mottling. Plants with this peculiarity are handicapped in the struggle for existence and thrive only under human care.

48 VEGETABLE IVORY (COELOCOCCUS)

A nut palm of the Polynesian archipelago produces these apple-sized, hard-shelled fruits. Their interior contains a seed of white color and stone-hard consistency. It is suitable for making carvings and these properties have given the seed its name of "vegetable ivory."

THE ANIMAL KINGDOM

49 TYPES OF RADIOLARIAN SKELETONS (RADIOLARIA)

This microscopic view shows but a small part of the multiplicity of forms displayed by the skeletons of radiolaria. These siliceous supporting structures occur mainly in spherical, annular or conical shapes in ever-new variations. Their lattice structure and their spikiness contribute to their harmonious appearance.

50 TWO RADIOLARIAN SKELETONS

This picture shows two main types of radiolarian supporting structures in great magnification: the cone and the sphere. In living animalcules they support a unicellular protoplasmic body, which constantly protrudes pseudopodia for the purposes of nutrition and locomotion. The outer layer of the animal also consists of protoplasm interspersed with many gas-filled vacuoles. This facilitates floating in the water.

51 SHELL OF FORAMINIFERA

Despite its appearance this shell is not a snail's shell but that of a tiny unicellular animal. The many pores (foramina) in the shell have given the group its name. The plasmatic body protrudes its pseudopodia through these openings. Foraminifera are exclusively marine animals; their shell is calcareous.

52 TORTOISE SHELL (TESTUDO)

The horny plates are easy to see on this back view of the shell, but they are its less important part. For below them is a solid armor of bone which surrounds the tortoise. The ridges of the horny plates are expansion layers, allowing for further growth of the plates corresponding to the growth of the bone structure underneath. The age of the animal, however, cannot be determined from their number.

53 CROSS-SECTION THROUGH THE SPINE OF A SEA URCHIN (ECHINIDAE)

Cross-sections through calcareous objects, such as sea-urchin spines, are not obtained by cutting, but by grinding and polishing. The extremely thin slices thus produced can be photographed under a microscope to obtain a picture of this kind. In this case calcareous prisms are embedded in a calcareous mass of a different system of crystallization to form a concentric column. From the outside the internal structure, which varies from species to species, cannot be inferred. Only longitudinal ridges are visible.

54 SKELETON OF STAR CORAL (ASTRAEA)

No name could fit these animals better than star corals. Every little star of the depicted calcareous skeleton was formed by a living coral polyp; in their entirety they formed a coral colony. Corals are coelenterates; their hollow inside is traversed by septa pointing towards the central axis: this increases the surface area for the digestive processes. The septa are supported by the lamellae visible in the picture.

55 SKELETON OF RED CORAL (CORALLIUM)

Red corals are colonies of animals whose branched body axis becomes calcified and thus acts as a supporting structure. The outer layer remains fleshy. Inside it are the polyps, connected with each other by small canals. The attractive red of this coral skeleton has been much prized by man since antiquity for its ornamental effect.

56 GLASS SPONGES (EUPLECTELLA)

These sponges have a skeleton consisting of fine siliceous tubes, one to two feet in length. At the far end of this tube, which is not visible in this picture, they are equipped with a cluster of strong siliceous needles which serve to anchor them at the bottom of the ocean, usually at depths below 1600 feet. The porous lid of the outlet opening (osculum) is visible. It resembles the spout of a watering can.

57 FAN OF VENUS (RHIPIDIGORGIA)

Horn with calcareous deposits is the material from which this coral skeleton is built. In life it is covered by a yellowish or purple body substance. These corals, with other species, form colored forests in shallow waters, some individuals reaching a height of three feet and a span of five feet.

58 HARP-SHELL (HARPA)

This snail shell with its lines, colors and shapes is a feast for the eyes. But its full beauty becomes apparent only after the death of the animal, because while the animal is alive its shell, like that of most marine snails, is concealed by a plain horny covering layer, the periostracum.

59 PIRULA SHELL

This snail shell owes its characteristic fig shape to the last convolution which is oversized in all dimensions. The surface gets its lattice effect from the broad spiral stripes and the fine longitudinal lines. The various irregularities near the seam round the opening are caused by growth disturbances due to external influences. They are not typical of the species.

60 ARMOR OF GIANT ARMADILLO (PRIODONTES)

Armadillos are well armored, both for hunting ants and especially for protection against enemies. For below the horny layer of the epidermis there is a bony layer formed by the dermis. The armor is articulated into head plate, shoulder plate and pelvic plate which are rigid. In between there are movable portions. The picture shows part of the shoulder plate with the lower part of the head plate.

61 TAILPIECE OF THE LYRE BIRD (MENURA)

Lyre birds are shy inhabitants of Australian forests, with a limited capacity for flight. Thus their mating display takes place on the ground, and the elegantly shaped lyre is brought forward over the head and spread. The main feathers, which give the impression of a lyre, are somewhat modified from the fundamental type. The shaft is bent and the outer parts of both feather vanes are degenerated.

62 BACK VIEW OF PEACOCK (PAVO)

This beautiful view of a peacock's back might be called a waterfall of feathers. It lies in front of the ornamental feathers that make up the fan-tail (cf. plate 81). The tail feathers are formed and replaced from the last feathers depicted in this portion. Near the end it can be seen clearly how a gradual development of the back feathers to the ornamental type takes place.

63 PADDLE FIN OF ICHTHYOSAURUS

Ichthyosaurs have been extinct for millions of years and remain only as fossils. They were reptiles adapted to aquatic life, with limbs transformed into fin-like paddles as shown here. A parallel development of originally different-looking organs leading to such similarity as that of the ichthyosaurus fin to the paired fins of fishes is called convergence. Contemporary mammals that have returned to aquatic existence, like the whales, underwent a similar transformation of their limbs.

64 TROPICAL FISH (PTEROIS)

Shallow reefs and rocks and coral forests of tropical seas are the preferred abode of these fishes. With their brilliant coloring in which no tone is missing they

18

fit in well there. They are slow swimmers, and flying (as their systematic name "volitans" seems to suggest) is quite outside their range. Their prickles are rightly feared: they are equipped with poison glands and cause painful wounds that are difficult to heal.

65 X-RAY PHOTOGRAPH OF SOLE (PLEURONECTES)

The flatfish of which the sole is one have an extremely flattened body, which is strongly asymmetrical, in adaptation to their existence near the sea-bottom. During their growth both eyes, with part of the skull, are shifted to one side, thus making a seeing side and a blind side. The blind side is usually unpigmented. Hand in hand with these external changes considerable inner rearrangements take place. This photograph shows chiefly the skeleton. The central cord of the vertebral column has spinal protuberances above and below. These spines are loosely connected with the fin ray-bearers on which the fin rays rest.

66 MALAGASY CHAMELEON (CHAMAELEO)

Chameleons are distinguished by a few remarkable anatomical and physiological peculiarities. Firstly they can move their eyes independently of each other. Secondly they possess sticky propelling tongues with which they can capture their prey with lightning speed without moving from their position. Thirdly their tails are prehensile. Moreover they have the ability to undergo intensive color changes. Since their movements are slow they are difficult to discover.

67 RUFF FEATHERS OF LADY AMHERST PHEASANT (CHRYSOLOPHUS)

The feather area of the head is reminiscent of the wigs of bygone centuries. It is part of the mating plumage of the cock and is thus a secondary sexual characteristic. During the mating display all the feathers of this portion are spread out from the body, which gives them the appearance of a ruff.

68 HONEYCOMB

The female workers of the honeybee (Apis) build combs of this kind for their young and for storage. The exactitude with which they work is hereditary and always leads to the same result. The wax used in building is produced by the animals themselves from glands on the lower side of their abdomen. It is shaped and worked by their mandibles. In cells like those depicted, worker bees are bred from fertilized eggs. The drones are bred from unfertilized eggs in larger cells. Queen cells are very large and bag-shaped. In them queens develop with special food from fertilized eggs.

69 SCALY ANTEATER (MANIS)

The scales of this animal resemble those of a fir cone in shape and arrangement. But unlike those of fir cones they consist of horn. They cover the upper surface of the body and the tail on all sides. The underside of the body and the inside of the legs are hairy. When they scent danger scaly anteaters can roll up into a ball.

70 FEEDING PATTERN OF A CATERPILLAR (PHYLLOCNISTIS)

Under the epidermis of this leaf the caterpillar of one of a small butterfly species has eaten a path for itself. The paler portions of the leaf show the extent of the feeding, the dark line is the fecal track of the animal. The animal's path is often prescribed by conditions: as it cannot bite through the larger leaf veins it has to follow such veins when it encounters them until a weaker vein is found. That leads to this characteristic pattern.—Feeding tracks below the leaf surface are called mines, in analogy to human activities. Their arrangement is usually characteristic enough to determine the species of the mining insect.

71 FEEDING PATTERN OF A BARK BEETLE (IPIDAE)

The female bark beetle gnaws passages into the bark or the wood of trees in which she deposits her eggs. The species responsible for the holes shown breeds in the bark. The larvae which hatch from the eggs gnaw their own passages. At the wider end of these they pass into the chrysalis stage. Two such pupa nurseries are to be seen in the upper part of the picture. The beetles which emerge from these nurseries have to gnaw their way through the bark to the outside again. This mode of life makes the bark beetle one of the most feared forest pests.

72 SHELL OF A SEA URCHIN (CLYPEASTER)

There are two groups of sea urchins, each with a fundamentally different symmetrical structure. The Regularia, which include the well-known spherical sea urchins, display five-radial symmetry, while the Irregularia, as in the form depicted here, are bilaterally symmetrical. The kinship of both forms is recognizable, however, in the quinquepartite flower pattern. The holes which make up this pattern serve to maintain communication between the tube feet of the animal and the water vascular system inside the shell which moves them.

73 SHELL OF WING SNAIL (PTEROCERA)

Wing snails are distinguished by a large and wing-shaped mantle edge. A few species have spiky or talon-shaped protuberances in addition which may serve to keep the shell anchored to the ground. These talons gave rise to the systematic name of the species, Pterocera chiragra, which means "gout-handed wing snail."

74 BRAZILIAN PEACOCK BUTTERFLY (CALIGO)

The colorful splendor of a butterfly's wing is due to the pigmentation of the little chitin scales which cover the wing like a powder. These scales are attached to the skin by little stalks, and from their arrangement the patterns and designs take shape, as the peacock's eye in the picture. Every time the wing is touched, sometimes even with strong fluttering, the delicate scales are lost in part or completely, impairing the beauty of the butterfly.

75 INDIAN WHITE BUTTERFLY (DELIAS)

The butterflies and moths are called lepidoptera because of the microscopically small scales (lepides) covering their wings (ptera). The color of the wing is a combination of the colors of the scales. These colors are due, usually and in the case of the white butterflies, to pigments contained in the scales. But there are also color effects which are produced merely by the structure of the scale surfaces, without the presence of any pigment in the scales.

76 GOLIATH BEETLE (GOLIATHUS)

The Goliath beetles are a kind of rose beetle. They occur abundantly in tropical countries, especially in Africa. Despite their plumpness and their considerable size —they measure about four inches—they are good fliers. The two sexes are easily distinguished by the presence of a fork-like protuberance on the head of the male.

77 BACK PLUMAGE OF OCELLATED TURKEY (MELEAGRIS)

The backside of this turkey species is resplendent with many colors. The cock strutting about at pairing time in the full splendor of his mating plumage and his other seasonal features presents a wonderful array of shapes and colors to the observer and a mating stimulus to the female.

78 SHELL OF MARINE SNAIL (NAUTICA)

This shell from the Mediterranean has numberless dark or red-brown dots on a light brown background. They are arranged in rows which follow the growth strips of the shell. In the living animal much of the shell is covered by the appendages of the foot. On the underside of the shell is an "umbilicus." It is the opening of a hollow spindle which serves as an axis for the convolutions of the shell.

79 PINIONS OF ARGUS PHEASANT (ARGUSIANUS)

This design reveals many different types of markings: rows of dots, punctations, stripes, eyes. Even the shafts of the feathers participate in the composition. The hundred-eyed monster Argus from Greek mythology has inspired the name of this bird and of many other animals with a multiplicity of "eyes."

80 TAIL FEATHERS OF EMU (DROMICEIUS)

Apart from specialized adaptations all feathers have the same structure. The feather vanes are supported by a stem. From this stem barbs branch off on both sides which in their turn give rise to barbules. On the side nearer the tip of the feather the barbules bear small barbicels which interlock with the barbules of the next barb. This helps the vanes to form a rigid single surface.

81 FANTAILING PEACOCK (PAVO)

The disk of a displaying peacock is an ornament of a peculiar kind. It is made up of long ornate tail feathers with strong stems, which can be erected or folded down. The eye portion is the only part of each feather which presents a closed surface. The remainder of the feather vanes are loose and open, which decreases the air resistance of the disk. Even so, great force is necessary for erecting it.

82 SHELL OF A PORCELAIN SNAIL (CYPRAEA)

The shells of these snails always have a brilliantly polished surface. For they do not form a periostracum; instead, backward outgrowths of the mantle cover the whole shell. When danger threatens the animal retracts all its soft parts into the shell. Only then and after death the eye pattern is revealed which has given this species its systematic name "argus."

83 TONGUE OF A SNAIL (BUCCINUM UNDATUM)

In the snail's mouth cavity is a tongue-like organ whose surface is covered with tiny chitinous bands bearing sharp teeth. These bands form the so-called radula. Our picture shows a cross-section enlarged 240 times. The radula acts like a rasp, chafing off bits of food. The structure of the radula varies among snails and thus aids in their classification.

84 FLANK OF THE PLUMAGE OF A FRANCOLIN (FRANCOLINUS)

This bird has the same markings, with slight modifications, on each of the feathers of his flanks. The shape of the feathers closely conforms to the fundamental type. The vanes, separated by the stem, and the barbs of the feathers are clearly to be seen.

85 RIGHT FRONT- AND BACK-WINGS OF SUMATRAN FIREFLY (HOTINUS)

The basic structure of both wings of this insect is the network of veins which gives them the rigidity necessary for flying. In addition these veins carry the blood vessels, tracheids, and nerves supplying the wings. The pattern of the network is characteristic of the species and can be used for determining and distinguishing insect species inside a group. In addition to the veins the front wing has an irregular cluster of dark dots on it, the arrangement of which is subject to variations.

86 PRINT OF A RIGHT THUMB

The lines of the finger tips vary in some way in every human being. This fact is the basis of police detection methods, and proofs based on it are accepted by the courts. Even after deliberate destruction of the lines they are restored again in the old form by healing.

87 FUR MARKINGS OF THE JAGUAR (PANTHERA)

This portion of the flank of the jaguar displays the fur pattern characteristic for this species: approximate quadrilaterals and dots. No element in this pattern is like any other. That is necessary for perfect somatolysis. This term signifies the way in which the shape of the animal seems dissolved, as it were, in its natural surroundings.

88 POSTERIOR VIEW OF ZEBRA (EQUUS)

The method chosen here for "dissolving" the outline of the animal employs stripes rather than spots. Somatolysis must always correspond to the habitat of the animal concerned. The pattern of the stripes differs much from individual to individual and is not typical of the species.

PLATES

2 SPIRAL' NEBULA

3 GASEOUS NEBULA

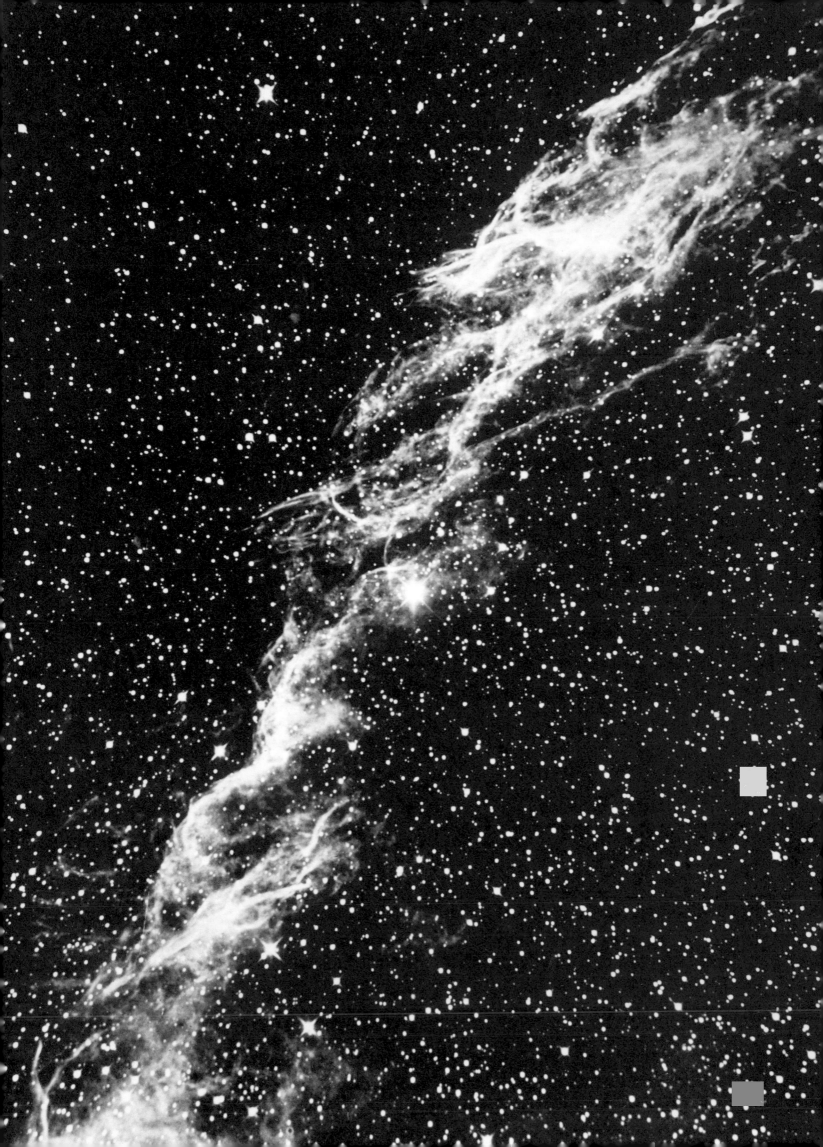

4   SOUTHERN PART OF THE MOON WITH CRATERS

5   FLEECY CLOUDS

6   FORKED LIGHTNING

8 DRIFT ICE AT THE COAST OF FRANZ JOSEPH LAND

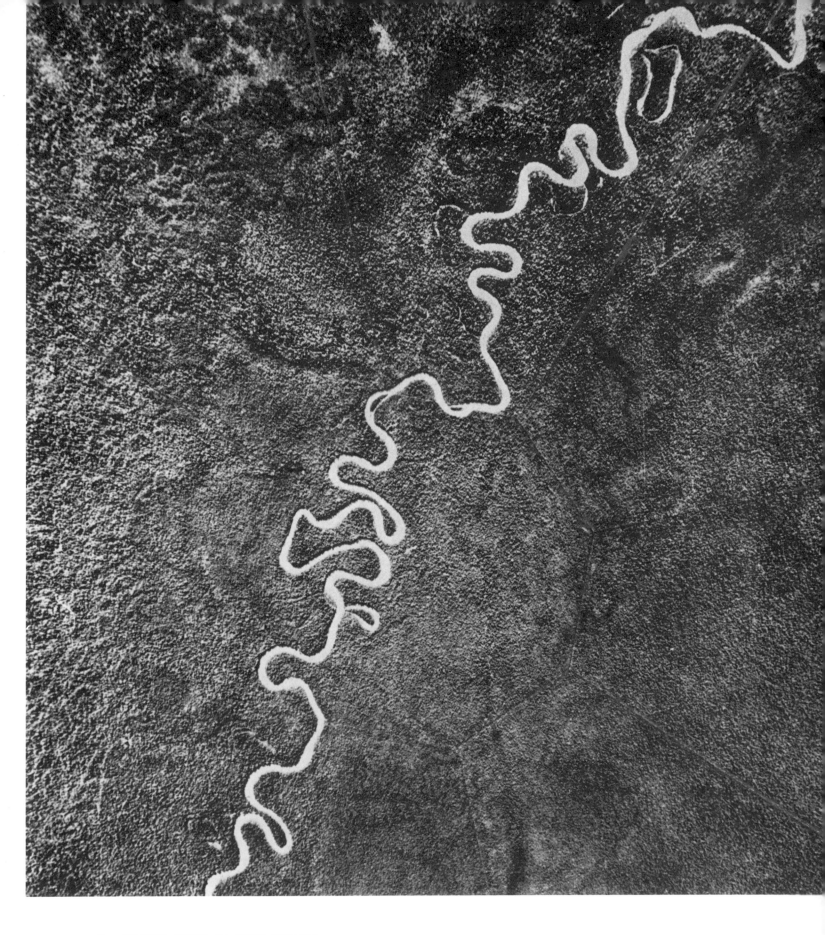

9   JUNGLE RIVER IN NEW GUINEA

10 COLORADO CANYON

11 SAND DUNES IN THE SAHARA DESERT

15   REFLECTION ON MOVING WATER

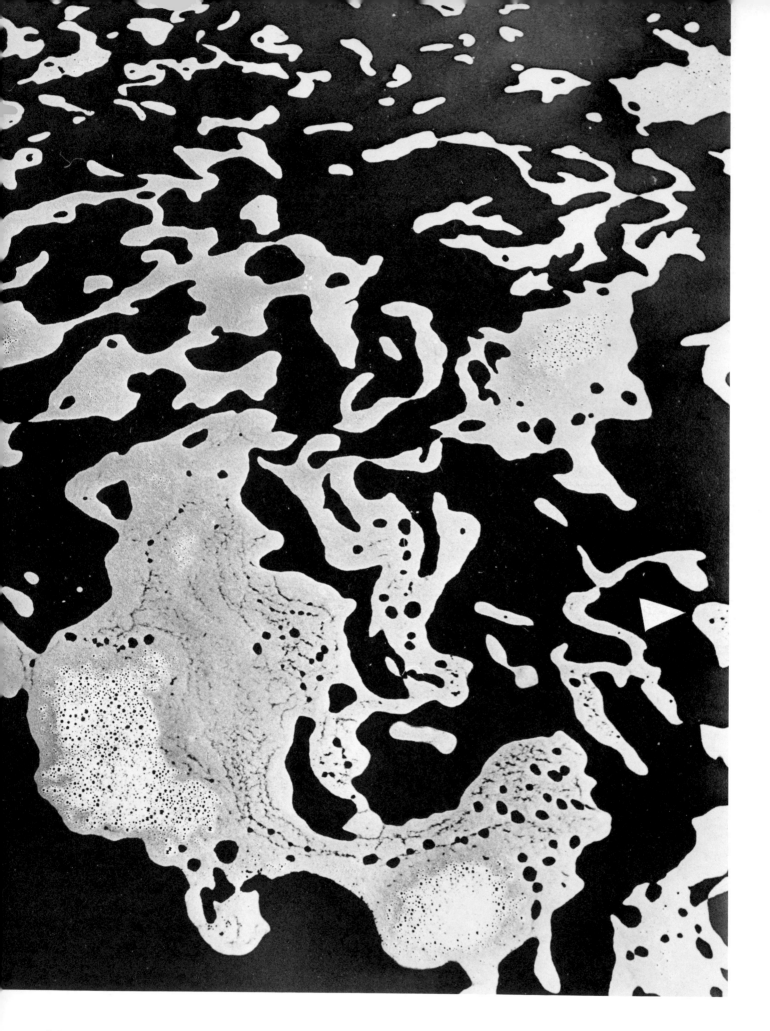

17   ROCK CRYSTAL

19 BASALT COLUMNS

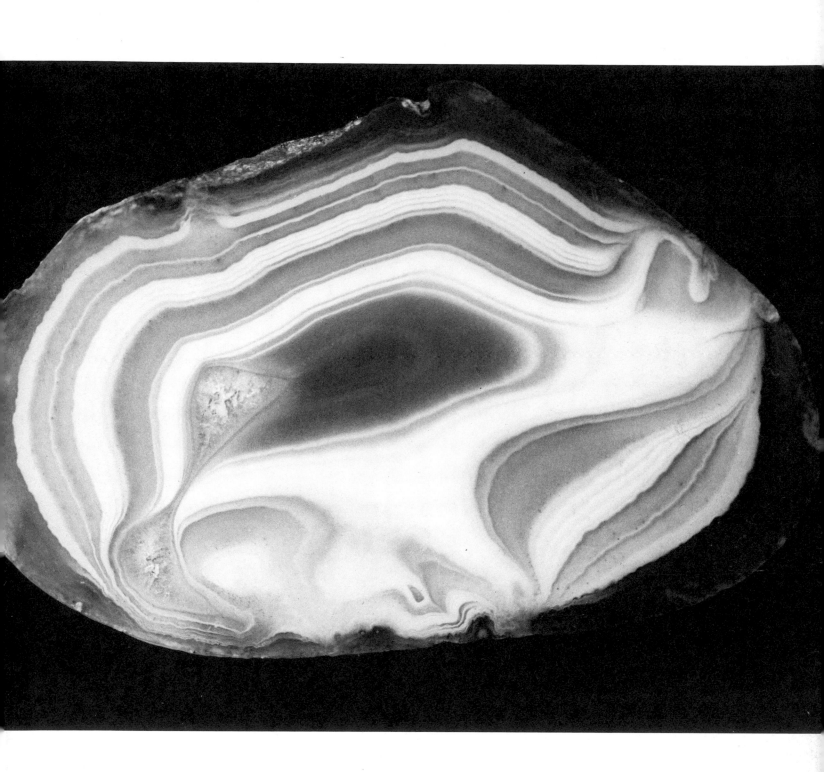

22 CALCSPAR CRYSTALS

24 VARIEGATED MARBLE

28 MENTHOL CRYSTALS

29 CRYSTALS OF SALT OF SORREL

31 METOL CRYSTALS

32　FROST CRYSTALS ON A WINDOW

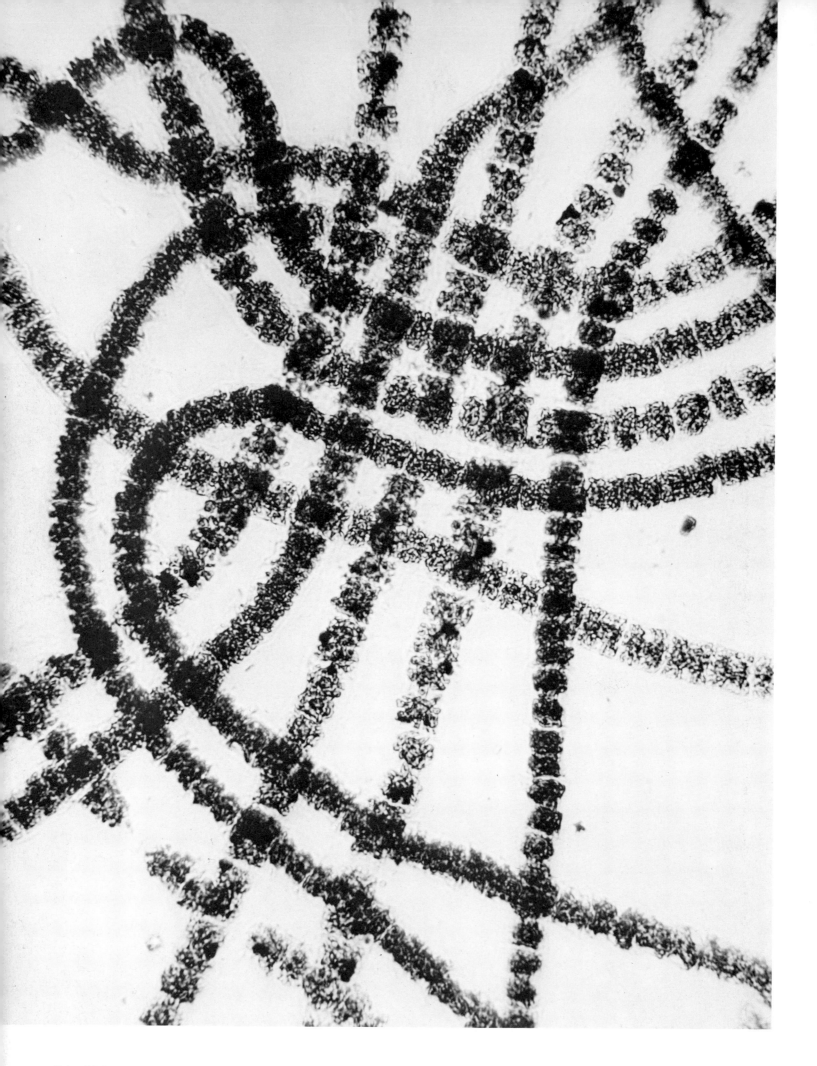

34   SPIRAL ALGAE

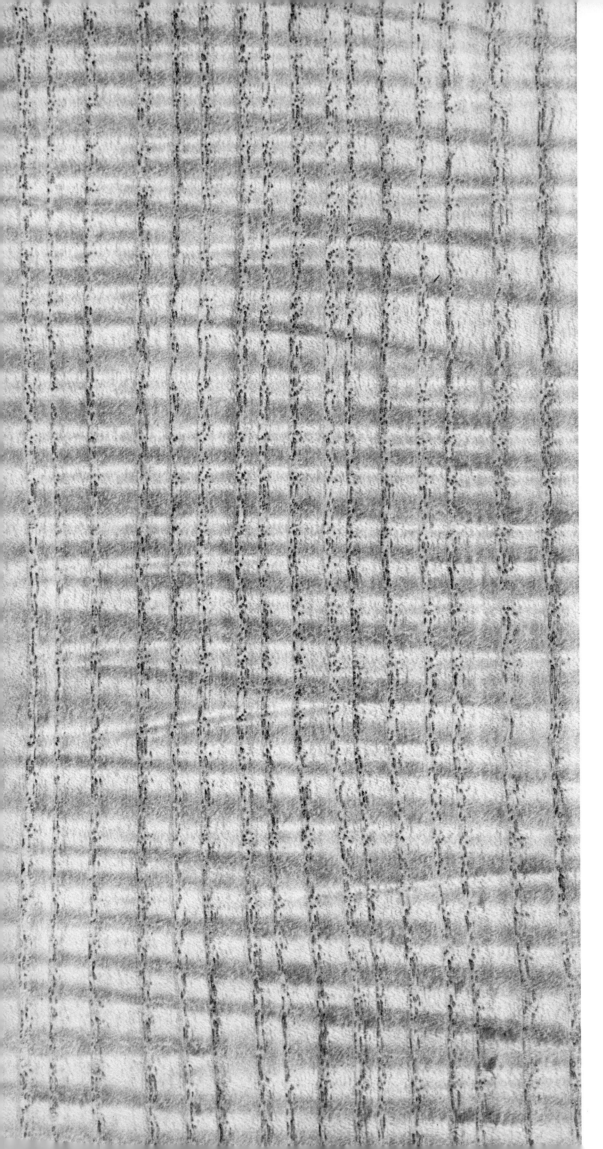

36 GRAIN OF ASH WOOD

37   CROSS-SECTION OF YEW TRUNK

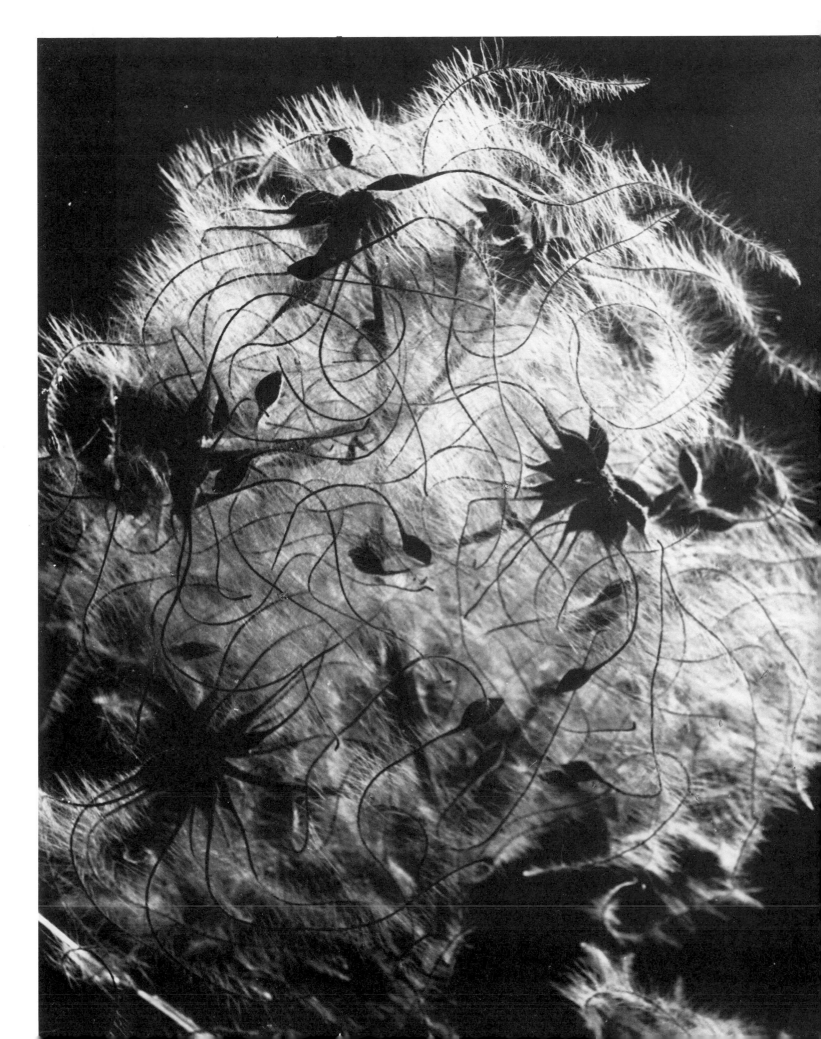

40 BEGONIA LEAVES

41 HOAR FROST ON STONECROP

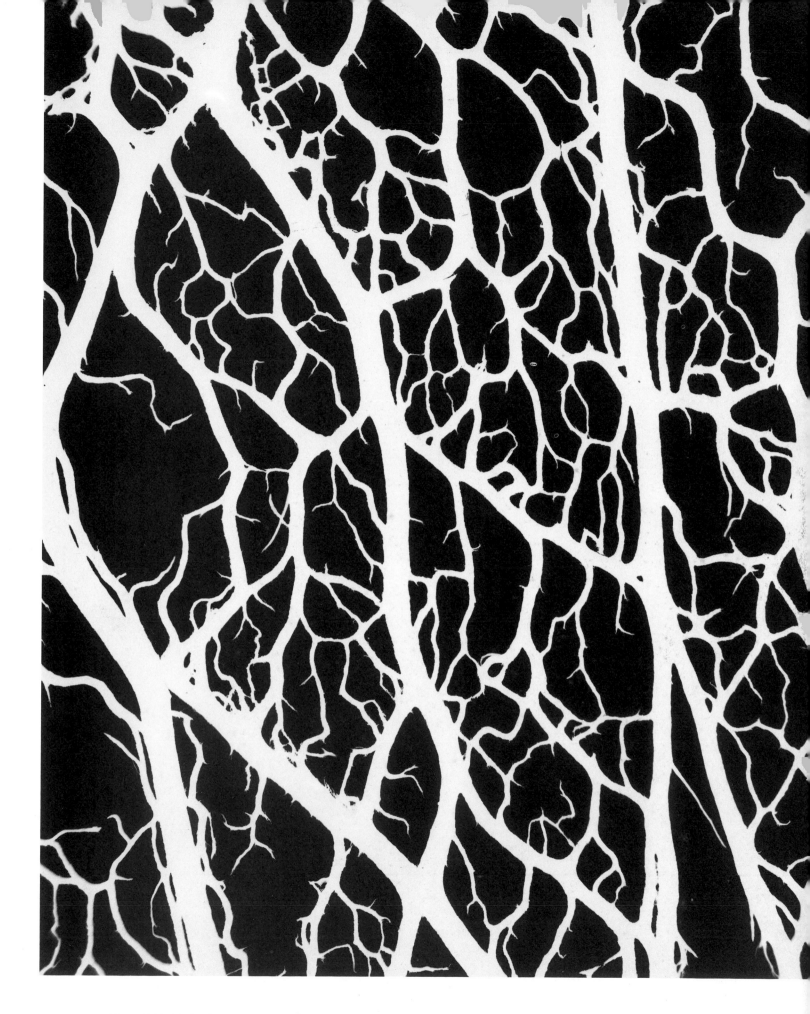

43   DECAYING ARTICULATION OF A PRICKLY PEAR

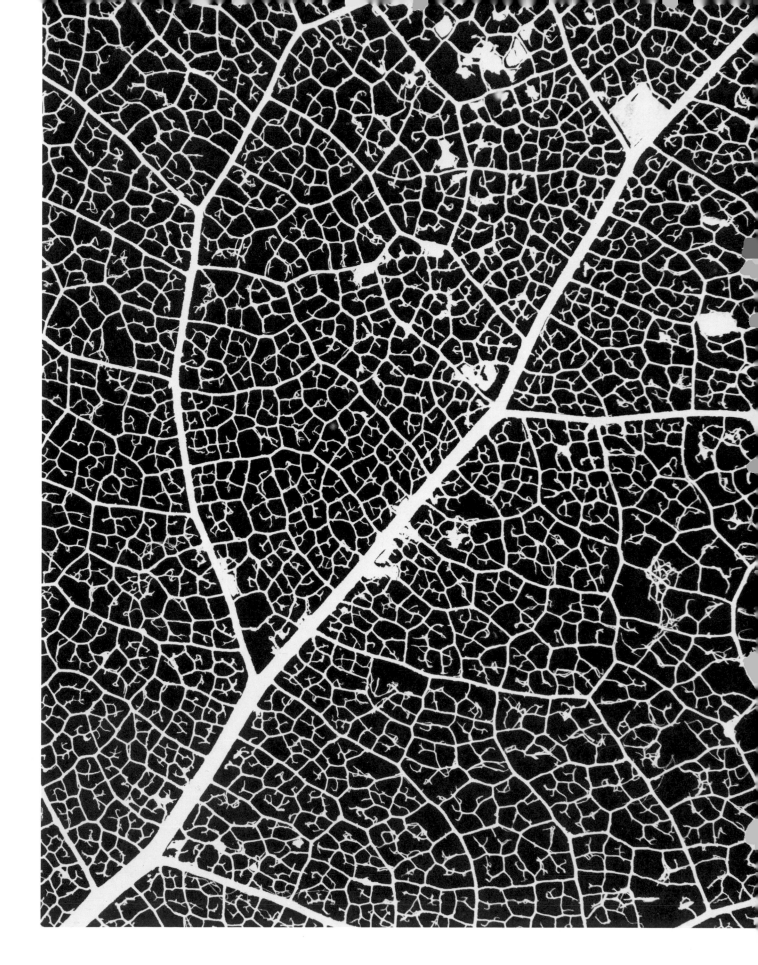

45   LEAF SKELETON OF THE BLACK POPLAR

44   BANANA LEAF

47   MOTTLED LEAF OF A BEGONIA

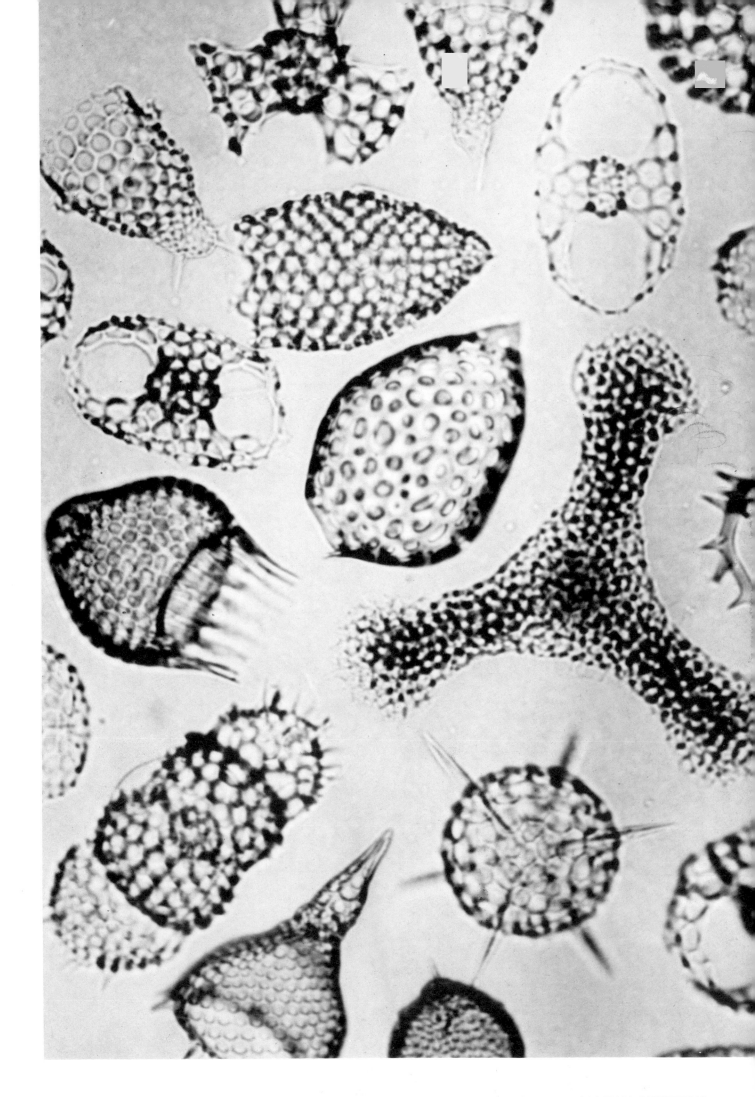

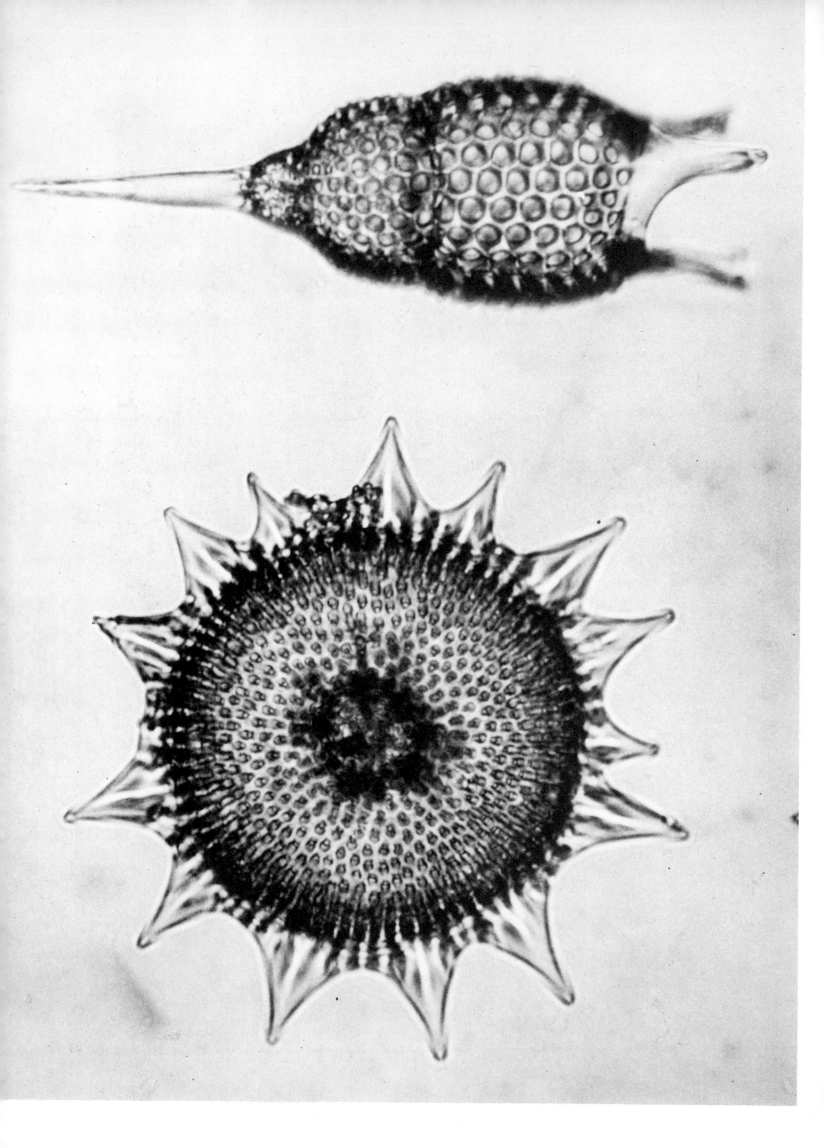

51   SHELL OF FORAMINIFERA

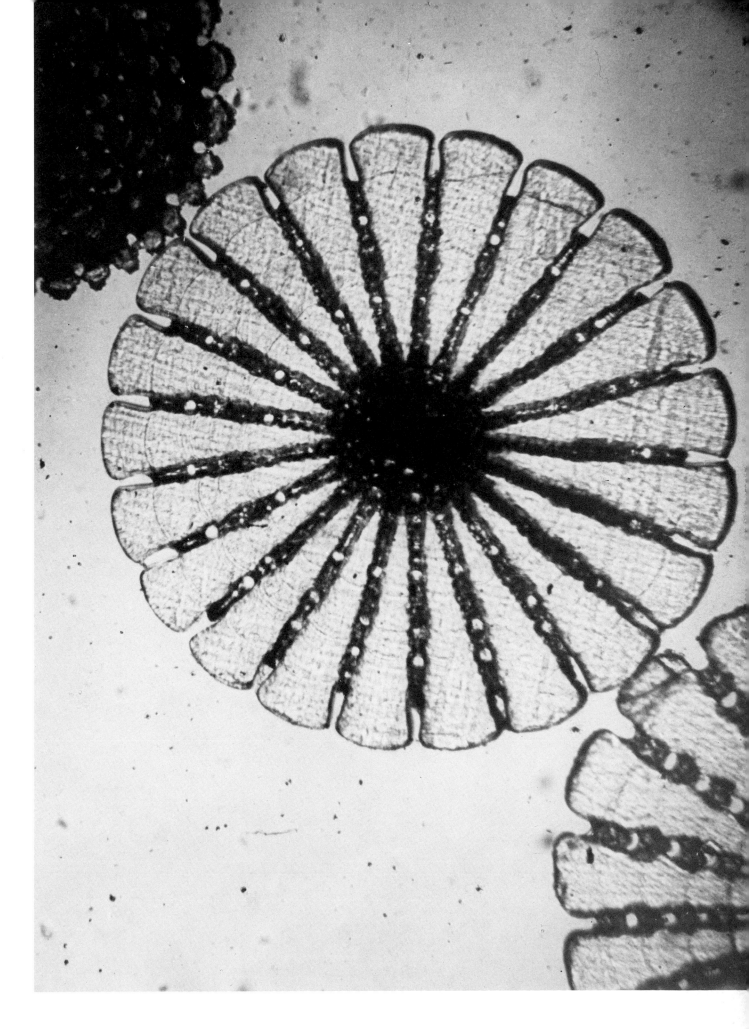

53 CROSS-SECTION THROUGH THE SPINE OF A SEA URCHIN

54   SKELETON OF STAR CORAL

55 SKELETON OF RED CORAL

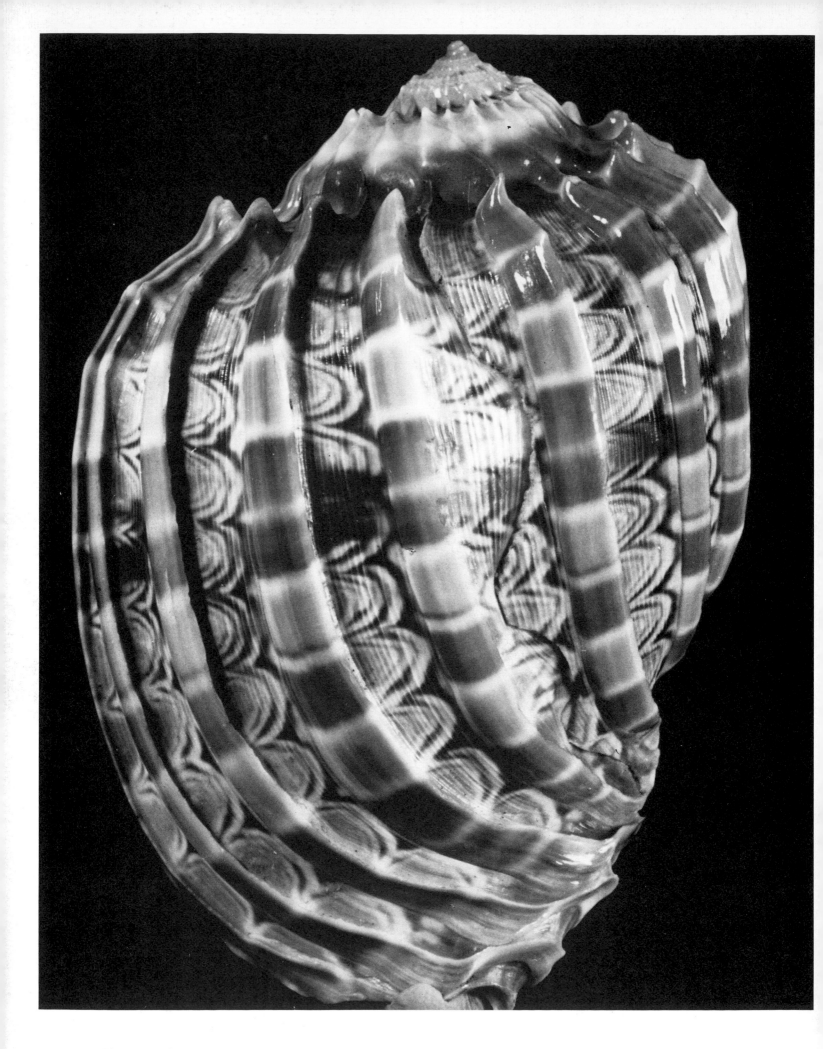

58 HARP-SHELL

63   PADDLE FIN OF ICHTHYOSAURUS

62   BACK VIEW OF PEACOCK

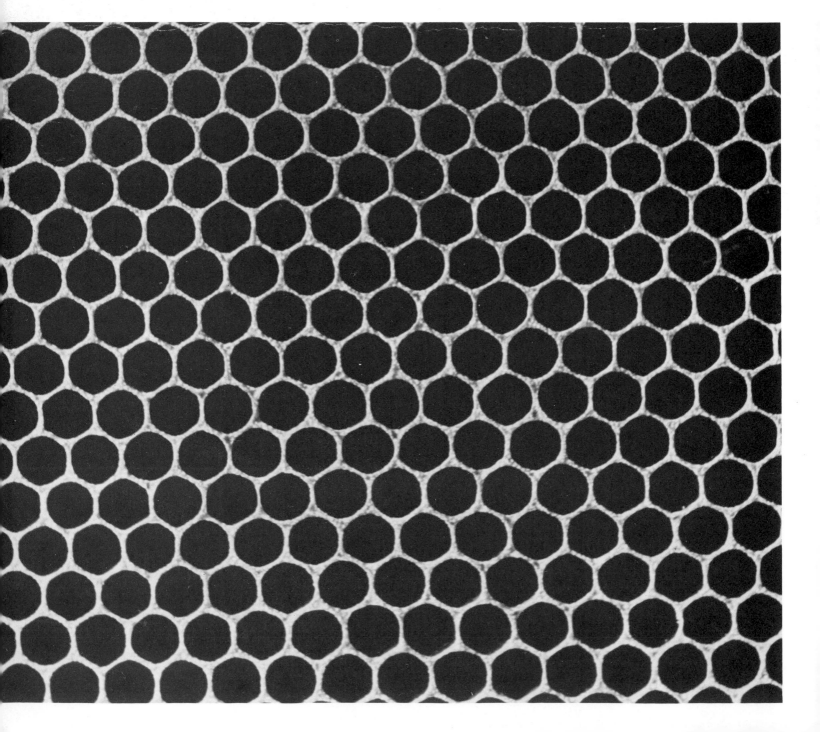

69 SCALY ANTEATER

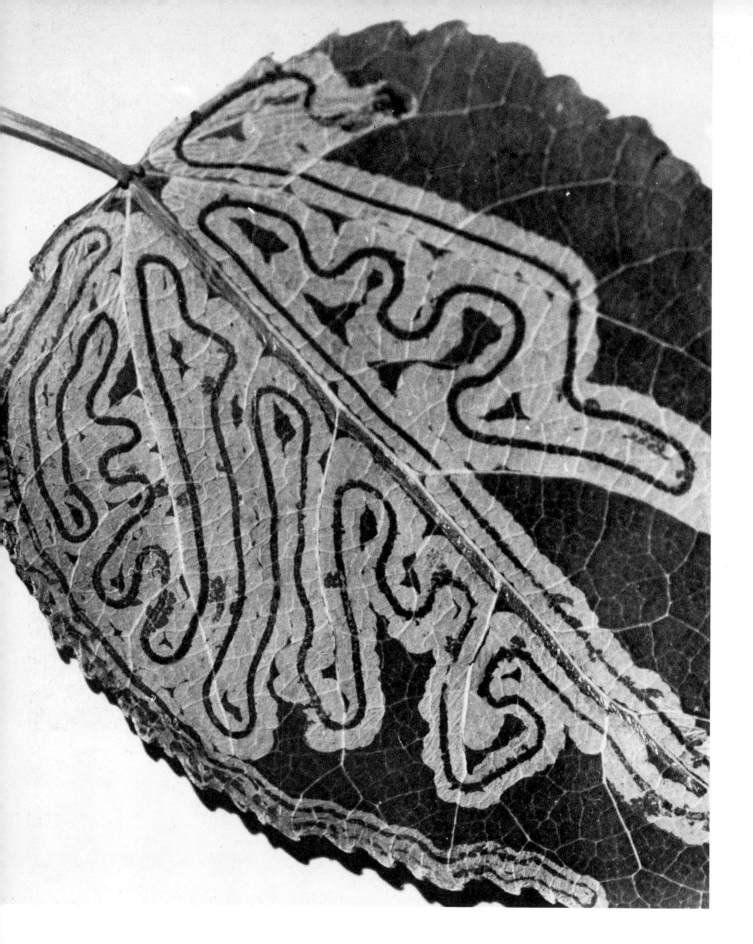

70   FEEDING PATTERN OF A CATERPILLAR

71   FEEDING PATTERN OF A BARK-BEETLE

72   SHELL OF A SEA URCHIN

75 INDIAN WHITE BUTTERFLY

74 BRAZILIAN PEACOCK BUTTERFLY

76 GOLIATH BEETLE

77 BACK PLUMAGE OF OCELLATED TURKEY

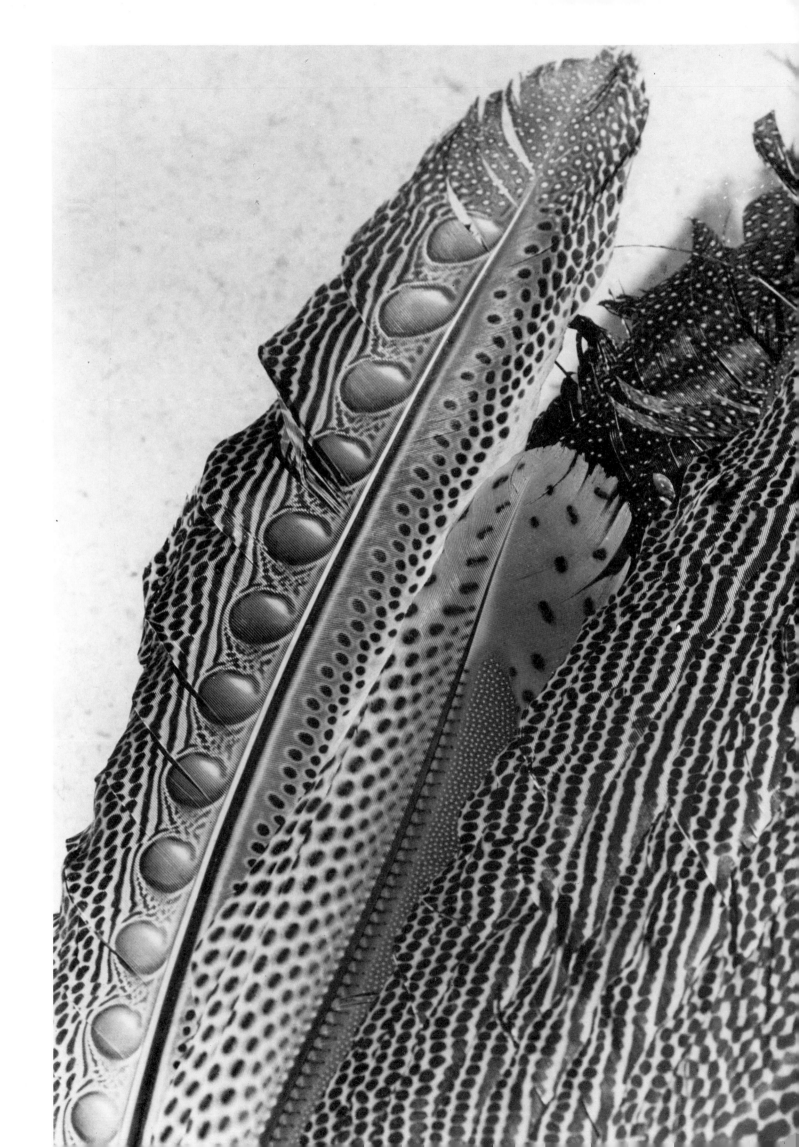

81 FANTAILING PEACOCK

82 SHELL OF A PORCELAIN SNAIL

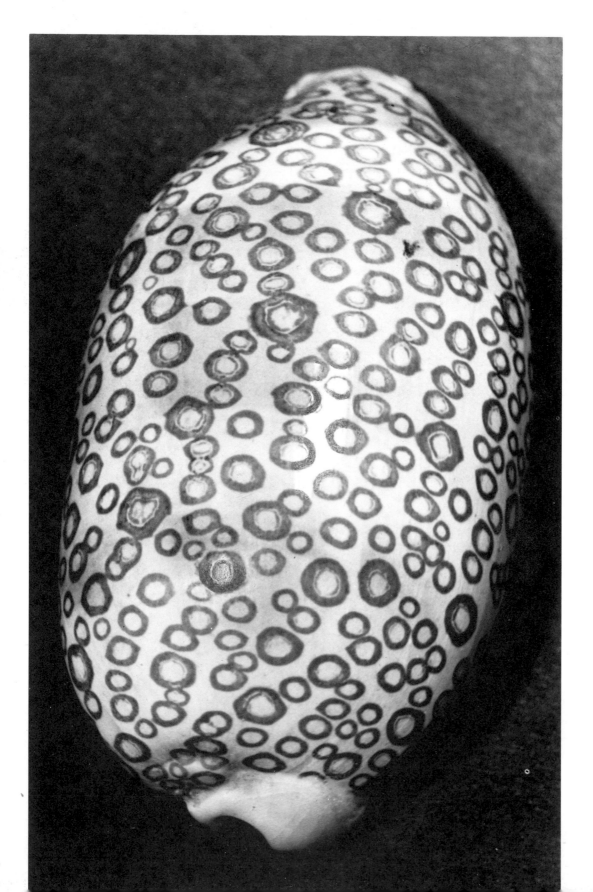

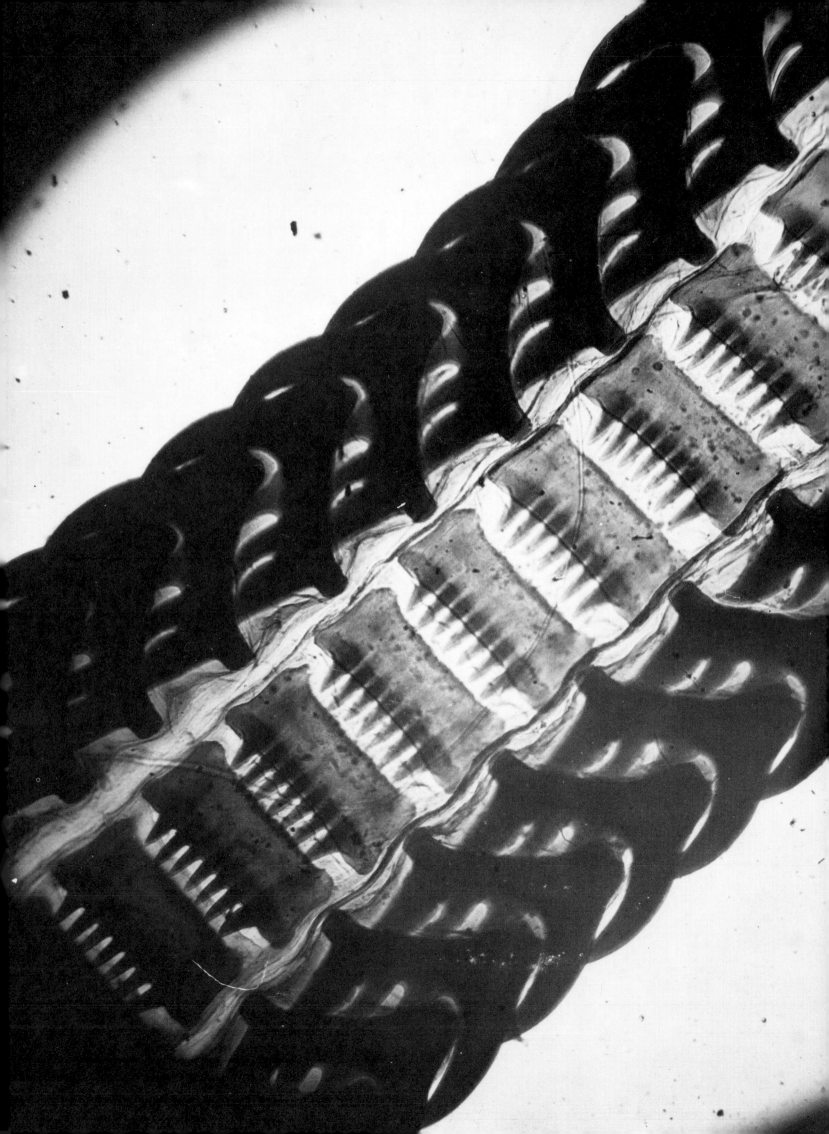

84 FLANK OF THE PLUMAGE OF A FRANCOLIN

85 RIGHT FRONT- AND BACK-WINGS OF SUMATRAN FIREFLY

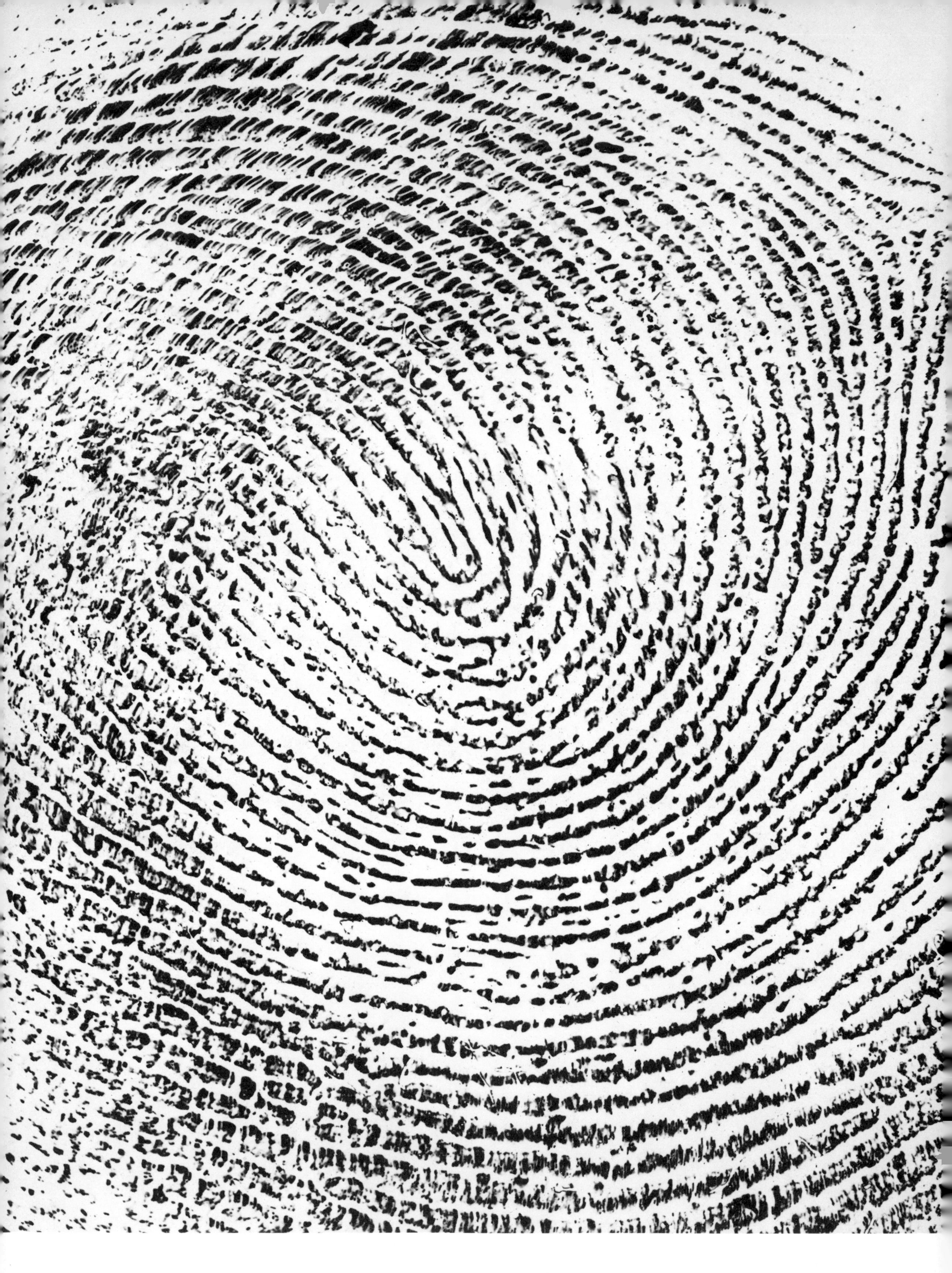

86 PRINT OF A RIGHT THUMB

87   FUR MARKINGS OF THE JAGUAR

Originally published by Pantheon in 1956, *Forms and Patterns in Nature* is a reissue of a marvelous collection of photographs of natural phenomena. The photographs reproduced in this volume reveal strikingly the harmonious shapes and formations created by nature in crystal, stone, plants, animals, in earth, water, constellations, nebulae, clouds. We see the structural pattern in bone tissue and in the cross-section of the spine of a sea urchin; the design in the stripes and spots of animal fur, in the plumage of birds, in the endless variety of shells, in the skeletons of coral, and even in the feeding patterns of bugs and caterpillars. These photographs bring to light the surprising likeness between the designs we find in nature and the patterns created in human art, particularly in modern abstract and geometric design. Along with the 88 full-page photographs, a detailed list of plates provides a scientifically accurate description of every subject.

Wolf Strache took most of the photographs in this book and has edited, since 1955, the *German Photographic Annals*.